Milestones and Memories

THE ART OF THE TOAST

STEVE DEYO

For my parents, Harold Deyo: 1915-1986
And Martha Deyo: 1921-1972

And to all the Americans killed on September 11, 2001 in New York City, Washington D.C. and Pennsylvania.

Memories are never perishable.

Milestones and Memories:
The Art of The Toast

This edition published by Aventura Communications
2003

Design by Heidi Domagala
Cover Photograph by Jared David Paul Anderson

Printed in the United States of America

ISBN 0-9719553-0-1

D 9 8 7 6 5 4 3 2

Acknowledgements

Great lives are led by those who give greatly of themselves and their time. There can be no greater gift than the gift of time. Time is our most valuable possession and I wish to express my thanks to those who have given this book their time.

Let me deliver a special thank you to Dick Curtis, whose expertise in wine led me down a new pathway. I am also grateful for the support, encouragement, and confidence of many friends. In particular, let me extend my appreciation to Lynda Beebe and John Gabel, for their sincere friendship. Howard Small, Liz Jurkowski, and Allen Sparkman all provided expertise in proofreading and editing. Thanks so much. I also extend my heartfelt gratitude to Heidi Domagala for her brilliance and creativity in the design and graphics shown throughout this book.

Finally, many thanks to the teachers in my life whose time, wit, and wisdom, served me so well in this endeavor. Without great teachers I would never have learned the importance of the life themes worthy of toasting. Teachers shape our lives and deliver the ultimate truths of life itself. Thanks to the teachers we can all lead great lives.

— Steve

Table of Contents

Table of Contents

Introduction

Life is like art, and therefore subject to many interpretations. During your life there will be milestone events that paint memories upon the canvas of your life. You are your life's original artist and the colors (memories) you select to cover your canvas are a reflection of who you are. Tell me what your favorite memories in this life are, and I will tell you who you are. We are, after all, what we do.

There is much to celebrate in life. There is much to experience. There is no better way to celebrate each milestone event than to lift a glass and pay tribute to a person, sentiment, or occasion. You see, an eloquent toast, like the stroke of the artist's brush, tells the story of how you feel at that particular moment. And many months, years and decades after your words have colored a moment, they can continue to illicit warm emotional reactions.

Toasts can be the links in which we tie all of life's experiences together. All of the many milestones in your life should be celebrated with someone toasting the event. From beginning to end, your life is a true miracle given to you by God. What you and I do during this sub-

Introduction

lime sojourn is our way of saying "Thank You" to God. Everyday of our life can be a great celebration. When you raise your glass and honor someone, some event, or some idea, you make the moment more memorable. It is an expression of style. It is a moment of mutual sharing and mutual delight. It is the highlight of any gathering.

In a world that seems increasingly discourteous, discouraging, and derogatory, you, the artist, daub on the positive emotions of happiness, health, gratitude, contentment, and most nobly, love.

Actually there isn't a week that goes by without some reason to raise your glass and salute someone you love. Take some time out of your hectic schedule, pause, and reflect on what is really important to you. Put your feelings into words and then tell that person, and all in attendance, how you feel. You'll be creating a long-lasting memory.

Make your memories monumental!

A Brief History

A Brief History

Making a toast is a little like making love — just a little bit shorter. From time immemorial, whenever family or friends have gathered together, there have been toasts made. When was the first crude vessel raised to honor an ancient god, an event, or someone? No one really knows. However, thanks to archaeologist Patrick McGovern, we know that winemaking dates to around 5400 B. C. McGovern, a professor at the University of Pennsylvania, found traces of red and white wine sediment in pottery shards from an excavation in the Zagros Mountains in western Iran. Suffice it to say that if the wine was flowing, then be assured, people were making toasts as well. Every time you and I "pop a cork" we're opening a bit of history — some 7400 years' worth!

Avid readers of the Bible know that the vine and its chief by-product, wine, are mentioned more often than any other plant or drink. Translations of the ancient Hebrew texts revealed that Noah loved making wine. Certainly, he lifted his "glass" to his wife and "guests" on that long boat ride. Homer, (not Simpson) wrote in the

Odyssey that Ulysses drank to the health of his hero, Achilles. We also know that the Greeks had a custom which involved a pledge of three cups to Mercury (a god of trade), Graces (a goddess of beauty), and Zeus (a god of rain). Was this a way of saying, "Give us enough rain to grow the grapes so we can sell our wine and keep our beautiful wife happy?"

About 2600 years ago the art of the toast really came into full swing. Those fun-loving Greeks used toasting as a way of symbolizing friendships. By pouring some wine into a drinking vessel, making a toast, and then drinking, the friend was assured that the wine was safe. You see, spiking wine with poison (arsenic, hemlock, lead?) did away with enemies, silenced competition, and prevented messy divorces. Definitely cheaper than lawyers, wouldn't you say? Ergo, toasting solidified families and friendships.

Next, came the Romans. Well, as we all know, the Romans liked just about everything the Greeks had in their society, and toasting was no exception. It seems that the Romans produced some pretty strong wine (even without poison!). So, to remove that bitter aftertaste, the Romans threw pieces of burned bread into the wine. The charcoal flavor reduced the acidity and made for a pleased palate. The Latin word *tostaré* (toes-tar-ray) which means roasted, or parched, is where we get the English word, toast! Over the centuries, this ritual of placing burned bread into the wine, evolved into the actual event itself.

If we fast forward to 1749, we first see the word toastmaster appear in the novel, *Tom Jones*. Written by British novelist, Henry Fielding, we learn that "a toastmaster presides over any special celebration and proposes, as well as, announces the toasts."

Taxes, tyranny, traditions, and of course, toasting came to colonial America with the British. It is probably no coincidence that America's first reported winery (1773) began its operation on the eve of the Revolutionary War. In addition, the Founding Fathers toasted our Declaration of Independence with some Spanish Madeira wine. For many years after our independence, it was the custom on the 4th of July "to raise a glass to honor each of the original 13 states." Yes, fireworks, a barbecue, and a round of toasts!

Toward the end of the 18th century there was a drinking club in London called the Anacreontic Society. Named for the Greek poet, Anacreon, who wrote about love and wine, the club ended each meeting with these words:

While thus we agree,
Our toast let it be.
May our club flourish happy, united, and free.
And long may the sons of Anacreon entwine,
The myrtle of Venus with Bacchus's vine!

Francis Scott Key liked the tune to this song so well that he used part of it when he wrote our Star Spangled Banner! Now, there's a real red, white, and blue connection between our country and the rich history of toasting.

And why not? Our ancestors valued the fine art of toasting. Toasting permitted them to honor important values. Values such as optimism, patience, imagination, courage, freedom, equality, justice, liberty, love of country, would make our nation great. Our ancestors recognized that strong values are what make make a great country, a great person, or a great organization. Our ancestors knew that when we lose values we lose our way.

One way to maintain our values is to maintain the art of toasting. A toast to a loved one, an event, or any type of milestone in your life is a symbolic gesture in praise of our values. A toast reminds one and all, of what you and I value about our nation, our family, and our friends. A toast has been, is, and will forever be, a love affair for all eyes and all emotions!

Milestones in Toasting

5400 BC	Approximate date of first winemaking from carbon dated pots found in the mountains of modern day Iran.
600 BC	Greeks establish "raising the cup" as a way of honoring and promoting friendship.
200 BC	Romans "toss on the taste" by placing piece of burned bread into wine cups.
900 AD	Norsemen of Northern Europe use skulls of their enemies as "cups" for toasting.
1709	The actual ritual of raising a vessel to honor a person, sentiment, or event takes on the name of "toasting."
1749	Henry Fielding writes the novel *Tom Jones* and we have the first "Toastmaster,"—one who announces and proposes toasts.
1776	The tradition takes on a new meaning as families propose toasts to the newly formed nation, The United States of America.
1920-1933	Prohibition deals toasting a setback.
1933-2001	Toasting limps along, since it is relegated to weddings, anniversaries, and state dinners.
2003	A renaissance begins with the knowledge that a toast celebrates life's special moments.

Toasting Days

Toasting Days

Every day can have its own memorable moment. Maybe you just found a new job, your spouse lost those ten pounds, or your daughter won the school spelling bee. These are all great reasons to create a memory. In addition, here a few days that deserve a toast during each glorious year:

New Year's Day	TO NEW BEGINNINGS
Martin Luther King, Jr. Day	A TOAST TO COURAGE AND FREEDOM
President's Day	A TOAST TO COURAGE AND FREEDOM
Valentines Day	A TOAST TO THE ONE WE LOVE
Easter Sunday	A TOAST TO PEACE, LOVE, AND KINDNESS
Mothers Day	A TOAST TO A WOMAN OF GRACE, ELEGANCE, AND CHARM
Memorial Day	A TOAST TO SACRIFICE, HONOR, AND DUTY
Fathers Day	A TOAST TO A MAN OF CHARACTER, COURAGE, AND CONFIDENCE

Toasting Days

JULY 4TH	A TOAST TO FREEDOM, COUNTRY, AND INDEPENDENCE
LABOR DAY	A TOAST TO WORK AND CONTRIBUTION
COLUMBUS DAY	A TOAST TO ADVENTURE, FREEDOM AND DISCOVERY
AUTUMN	A TOAST TO FOOTBALL, BURSTS OF COLOR, AND APPLE CIDER
THANKSGIVING DAY	A TOAST TO BOUNTY, FAMILY, AND BLESSINGS
CHRISTMAS DAY	A TOAST TO CHILDREN'S EYES, LIGHTS, AND FAMILY

Thoughts that Refresh

Nothing raises your social standing more than being a great gift giver — of toasts. If eloquence is "speech on fire" then you will always be regarded as the person to turn to when it comes to memory-making. When you are a host, say for a dinner party, try this: start with the guest of honor, and then go around the table telling something unique and wonderful (add the spice of humor) about each individual. Everyone should be laughing and loving your amusing commentary thrown in their direction. Your gift-giving will be so appreciated by all, that they will leave the table realizing that life is a celebration and you help to make it so. Do this each time you have guests and you will always have good company and companionship.

Passion

Passion

The first stage in any toast is passion. A toast must have passion. Passion educates us. Passion enlightens us. Passion entertains us. Passion sets the stage for eloquence. You must ask yourself several questions when you begin to write your toast: 1) What is it that gives me joy? 2) What is it that excites me about this moment? 3) What is it that makes my heart sing with happiness about this event?

Take some time and write down your thoughts. This will be the fuel that is needed to inspire you to deliver a toast that will help everyone to savor the moment and relish the memory. Every toast can be an everlasting memory for all who have gathered. To make each toast more memorable, you must have passion. The winds of chance and circumstance can take you anywhere, yet the words spoken that day will be forever a part of you. There is no better memory machine than the human brain. There is no better way to record the event than through the passionate words we speak. There is no better way to share your love, your care, and your person.

Preparation

Preparation

Now, that you've got that passionate fuel traveling through your veins, it's time for the second stage of your toast — ***preparation.*** A toast is really just a mini-speech. Toasts are to speeches as poetry is to novels: shorter and less complex; but just as moving. You have three aspects in preparation: a ***theme,*** a ***goal,*** and ***organization.***

THEME

Your theme can be a quotation, a phrase, a value, a vision, a strength, or an outstanding quality. The theme is the main foundation for your creative toast. Once you have chosen a theme, the remainder of your remarks should support, amplify, and be consistent with the theme. One might begin by saying, "As the Pulitzer Prize winning poet, Robert Frost once said...," and add the specific quote. You capture the essence of the toast with the theme. Oh yeah, just one other thought, there are no dull themes, just dull people.

GOAL

Where do you wish to take your audience? What should your message be? How would you like your words to be remembered?

Preparation

Every toast has a goal because for the next 1-3 minutes you're going to be taking the listeners on a short journey, and the goal is the destination.

ORGANIZATION

Each toast, like any presentation, has a beginning, middle, and an end. All three are important, but the middle is the most important. In the middle you will talk about personal experiences, tell a short story, give some concrete illustrations, have visual aids, and also humor. Humor is not optional. It is a requirement for most audiences. We all like to be entertained. Get a hold of a joke book, watch David Letterman, Jay Leno or Comedy Central. Change the wording a little to match your theme, and "Voila!" watch those happy faces! Say, for instance, you wish to salute the newest adventure of a co-worker:

> "Well, I've known Kenny for several years and his idea of an adventurous life is eating trail mix and watching the Discovery Channel."

Preparation

Your daughter just graduated from law school?

> "Cathy, you have finally reached your goal that you told me about all those years ago. You said, 'Dad, I want to be a lawyer because we live in a country for the lawyers, by the lawyers, and of the lawyers.' Now, go get some clients!"

The whole idea is to tell your tale without "putting the customers" to sleep. If you're smiling and getting the people to laugh, nobody will ever fall asleep.

Presentation

Presentation

Ready, for the third stage of the toast? This is the best part — the presentation. The most effective presentation has two ingredients: 1) you, the toaster; and 2) your attitude. To stir up your listeners, you must be stirred. What is it about this person, this occasion, or this moment that really excites you? We cannot inspire, motivate, or move the audience unless we are first inspired, motivated, and moved. Great wine comes from the harvest of great grapes. The same is true for toasts. A great toast comes from great ***gestures, voice,*** and ***words.***

GESTURES

Gestures supplement words and give your listeners something to look at while they listen. We all need to have a few gestures in our toasts — unless you're a supermodel or a movie star. In that case, then, "you don't need no gestures." For the rest of us, gestures with our arms, hands, fingers, face, and eyes are critical.

The use of gestures adds life to your toast. Keep this in mind: it's not possible for the average homo sapien to overdo them. In fact,

Presentation

9 out of 10 of us need to increase our physical activity according to the FGA — the Federal Gesture Association.

> Drink to me only with thine eyes
> And I will pledge with mine;
> Or leave a kiss but in the cup
> And I'll not look for wine.
>
> Ben Jonson, poet

The immortal words of Mr. Jonson sum up the toaster's eye contact for your toast. Before you begin, choose two people (besides the person you are toasting) to speak with. These people are your supporting "cast members." Try to have one to your left and the other on your right. Your cast members want you to do your best and they will support you with their friendly smiles and attention. In the beginning, the middle, and the end of the toast, your eyes will meet theirs (and the person you are toasting) many times.

After you have the audiences attention, wait five seconds, keep those eyes up, and begin your toast. Once you begin, move your eyes to your supporting cast from time to time. All this eye contact may be somewhat intimidating. However, the more you speak "with your eyes," the more successful your toast.

There are no "born toasters." Follow three rules: Rehearse; Rehearse; and Rehearse.

VOICE

How we use our voice in the toast is the second most important aspect of your presentation. Do we speak with a high voice or do we sound like Darth Vader? Do you sound like a barker selling half price tickets at a carnival ride or are you slow and deliberate like a sedated accountant? Maybe you throw in a French accent or assume the voice of your favorite cartoon character? No one is suggesting that you make any voice alterations for your toast. Not at all. These are just examples of different voices and how the listener might recognize them. As a matter of fact, if you are truly excited about the memory that you are creating, it will come out in your voice naturally. And that is the whole idea, right?

Each of us has been given our own unique voice. No one on the planet has the same voice as someone else. It's one of our distinguishing characteristics. All we're saying is this: How you say your toast plays a major part in its overall acceptance. Making a toast is like having a conversation with one person. Here are three tips to using that attractive voice that you have:

1. Be conversational — pretend that you are speaking with just one person.
2. Be sincere — speak from your heart and be yourself.
3. Be natural — never project an image to impress others.

Presentation

An exercise that you might try is to change the pitch (high or low) level of certain words. You can do this by placing a greater emphasis on different words. The *italicized* word should stand out.

May you *never* lack for friends,
Nor a glass of wine to *share* with them.

She is a person who *sparkles* with spirit,
A *woman* of profound intellect;
A *human being* of *supreme* compassion,
And a *wife* filled with kindness.

A *warm* toast
Good company
And a *glass* of wine
May you *enjoy* all three.

Presentation

Words

We are losing our verbal culture. Our perceptions are a result of the images shown on TV screens, computers, and Hollywood films. Words have always been the way for all humans to communicate. Words are what separate us from the animals. It is indeed lamentable that so much of our language today is characterized by profanity and vulgarity. Profanity is a detriment and a deterrent to quality thinking and therefore, has no place in any toast.

Words are the living monuments to the power of a toast. The words we use build anticipation and bring life to your toast. You want to use strong, sturdy, solid words. Your words need to be descriptive — words that paint pictures.

Instead of saying, "Bill was running as fast as he could," say, "Bill ran as fast as a cheetah at lunchtime." "Do lobsters grow on trees? Does caviar come from cactus? Does he have the appetite of a Komodo dragon?" Or maybe, "like a seafarer of old, traveling without charts, she sailed off toward terra incognita."

Presentation

The listener wants you to speak to their eyes. By using such colorful, vivid, and descriptive wording, you will add immensely to their perception of the moment. On top of that, you may just be referred to as a living, breathing, walking legend in the world of toasts!

So there you have it. Three simple stages. Now, for success, don't forget to rehearse, rehearse, and rehearse. Rehearse until it becomes "impromptu." Maybe that's 10 times and maybe that's 50 times. You be the judge. Great communicators rehearse and so do great toasters. You'll see and you'll succeed. Good Luck!

Seven Essentials of Toasting

Seven Essentials of Toasting

1. **THEME**
   The foundation — a quote, phrase, value, vision, strength, or outstanding quality.

2. **GOAL**
   The final destination of the toast — where you're taking the listener.

3. **ORGANIZATION**
   A beginning, middle, and an end.

4. **GESTURES**
   Your eyes, facial expressions, hands, arms, and overall body language.

5. **VOICE**
   Your pitch can be high, low, fast, slow, or with an accent.

6. **WORDS**
   Colorful, descriptive words that paint pictures for the listener.

7. **YOU**
   To inspire, motivate, and entertain, you must be inspired and motivated.

Sample Toast

Sample Toast

Based upon the information you have just read, let's put together a toast. Say that you want to honor a dear friend at a dinner party. This person's friendship has meant a lot to you, so the first stage, ***passion*** is already a given. Next, we go into ***preparation:***

THEME

"Friends are life's greatest treasure." By C. M. Russell

GOAL

To tell the audience know how important this friend has been to you.

ORGANIZE

Give examples of the friendship: specific instances, attributes of a true friend, humor, and maybe a visual aid.

The presentation might go something like this:

"Ladies and gentlemen, (with calm authority) I want to tell you about my very dear friend, Lynda. C. M. Russell, the great western artist, said that, 'Friends are life's greatest treasure.' If that is true, (pause) and I believe it is, (pause) then Lynda has been the gold standard (descriptive) in friendship for me. Right after my divorce, I went to Lynda and said, "I'm feeling so depressed today." She replied, "Why is that, Steve?" "Oh, it's just that sometimes I feel so alone and useless," was my answer. Lynda then said, "Steve, you don't have to feel so alone. A lot of people think you're useless" (pause for the laughter).

She always listened to me and all the problems I had with my children. She called me on holidays and worried about my eating the right foods. She always gave me suggestions, not advice, in dealing with my divorce. Lynda has the ability to make a person reflect, contemplate, and see the big picture (emphasize). She gave me this book (show the book, so that all can see) to read when I was down and out. Most of all, she accepts me for who I am and respects me as a human being. Now, (emphasize) that's a true friend —

someone who sees through you, and still enjoys the view (painting a picture). Lynda, my friend, you are a true treasure, and I thank you for all your kindness. Ladies and gentlemen, (pause) please raise your glasses and join me in saluting my friend, (pause) Lynda."

See, it's not that hard. Just follow the formula. You can do it!

Length

Length

As we've said, a toast is really a mini-speech, so it's length is also abbreviated. Being eloquent usually requires, oh, say, at least 30 seconds, right? Sure, and most memory-creating words may go up to three minutes or so. In that span you can bring laughter and tears to the eyes of anyone listening. Much more than three minutes and you're heading into the "Greer Garson" zone. In 1942, Greer Garson won the Academy Award for Best Actress for her role in the movie *Mrs. Miniver*. At 5 minutes and thirty seconds, her acceptance speech, remains, to this day, the record. According to historians, Ms. Garson had everyone in that audience begging for mercy.

EQUIPMENT

Two pieces of equipment: A liquid and a vessel to hold the liquid. For liquids:

Wine	Beer	Champagne	Water
Spirits	Soda	Juice	Milk
Coffee	Tea	Eggnog	Punch

Some unacceptable liquids:

Gravy	Mouthwash	Brake fluid

Etiquette and Protocol

Etiquette and Protocol

There are certain and accepted standards of behavior when giving or receiving a toast. Some of these may seem like "common sense," but as a sage once remarked, "Sometimes common sense isn't so common."

1. ***Always stand*** when offering your toast. It helps to get everyone's attention and most people will respectfully be quiet. No need to tap your wine glass — it might break. Don't laugh, it has happened!

2. ***The person/persons being toasted remain seated.*** Everyone else stands. Once the toast is finished, the person being toasted does not drink from his or her glass. This would be the equivalent of patting yourself on the back. You can merely say, "Thank you," or, since everyone will be in the mood, return the favor with your own complimentary toast.

3. ***The host is the first to toast*** the guest of honor. Now, if the host is shy or doesn't wish to offer a toast, then, you can politely request that you would like to do the honor.

4. ***It's not a good idea to push someone*** to make a toast who is uncomfortable in doing so. The audience may hear something they might not like to hear.

5. Always ***be polite and participate in a toast.*** You don't drink adult beverages? That's okay, it's perfectly acceptable to drink something non-alcoholic or even use an empty glass.

6. When you sit at the table, ***wait and watch.*** Wait before you drink from your wine glass. Watch to see if the host or hostess drinks from their glass. If they do, then they're not planning on giving an opening toast to their guests.

7. Leave any and all ***"locker room" comedy out*** of your commentary.

A Wedding Toast

A Wedding Toast

What do you say to your daughter when she begs you, beseeches you, implores you to not get too "windy" with your toast? Well, Dad, it's certainly true that this is your little princess's day and you want to make sure that she's happy. However, ask yourself this question, "I wonder who's paying for this memory?" If the answer is you, Dad, then you need to get your money's worth — and make some history with a toast that will last a lifetime. Here's the toast that this writer delivered on my daughter's day:

> "Today is Robin and Allen's celebration. It's a moment that they will remember all of their lives. Now, they have suggested that I should keep my speech short (yeah, right, under my breath) so you can enjoy the day with them. I'm sure that they didn't mean it quite like that — at least I'm almost sure. To all of you, I say, thank you so much for being here. We are very delighted to share this day with so many cherished friends and relatives from both families. For those of you who may not know Robin very well, I can tell you that she is a daughter to be proud of. Yes, of course, I'm biased. She does have a mind of her own — as I dare say Allen has discovered. When Robin was seven

years old we were on a camping trip in Montana. Dressed in her bib overalls that had a bright red handkerchief (I turn around with my posterior facing the audience showing MY red handkerchief!) embroidered on the back pocket, we walked along a tributary of the Yellowstone River.

Suddenly, she picked up a rock and was about to "skip it," when she stopped and asked, "Dad, will this kill a fish?" I said that it wouldn't, and I thanked her for her compassion and thoughtfulness. That's Robin.

As for Allen, he's kind, considerate, respectful, and filled with spirit. All necessary qualities for having a wonderful marriage. So, I'm sure that you'll all agree that I could do no better than to give them, from all of us, the old Gaelic blessing:

May the road rise to meet you,
May the wind be always at your back,
May the sun shine warm upon your face,
The rains fall soft upon your fields.
And until we meet again, may God hold you
In the palm of his hand.

Ladies and Gentlemen, please stand and raise your glass and drink a toast to the health, happiness, and harmony of this new couple. To Robin and Allen!

That was probably around three minutes in total, and barring all immodesty, the audience loved it. Afterward, my daughter's college age friends, as well as many parents congratulated me. I thanked them for their kindness. You know what? I never revealed how great it made me feel. This is a memory every father needs to carry throughout his life.

You see, this was a milestone in my life, too! My goal (and your goal too, Mom and Dad) was to spread the joy in all directions so that everyone in attendance that day will also have a fond memory. And that's what your toast can do.

Event Etiquette

ENGAGEMENT PARTY

The Toasters and order of appearance:

1. Father of the Bride
2. The Groom

Once all the glasses are filled, the father of the bride to be should stand, lift his glass and begin his toast. It can be as simple as, "I think that we should all drink to the health of Paula and the man she has chosen to become a permanent member of our family, Roy." Now, Dad, if you wish to use some of your newly developed skills that we've already discussed, by all means proceed. Everyone except the bride and groom rise. Next, if the groom has the guts (and he surely should!), he should express his own sentiments, as well as thank the hosts for the party in their honor.

WEDDING REHEARSAL DINNER

The Toasters and order of appearance:

1. Groom's Father
2. The Best Man

The groom's father makes a classy toast along the lines of, "My wife, Christy and I would like to ask you to join us in drinking a toast to two very lovely people, Paula's mother and father, Mr. and Mrs. Brown." The man making this toast has an ideal opportunity to express his sincere appreciation for the efforts, both physical and financial, of the bride's parents. The best man's toast ought to have a little humor about the groom and then a comment about how fortunate they each are to have found one another.

WEDDING RECEPTION

The Toasters and order of appearance:

1. Best Man
2. Groom to the Bride, parents, family, friends
3. Bride to Groom (optional)
4. Father of the Bride
5. Groom's Father
6. Mother of the Bride (optional)
7. Mother of the Groom (optional)

While the best man begins the toasting, Dad, (father-of-the bride) you are the toastmaster today! That's right, you took out a second mortgage, you've been a referee, and you've been tormented by a caterer who's aggressive, arrogant, and annoying. Yes, Dad, you've paid your dues and now it's your turn to dazzle the audience. Yes, this is your milestone, too!

If it's a sit down meal, wait until everyone has been served the first course and their glasses have been filled. For a standing reception, toasts are offered after everyone has gone through the receiving line and drinks have been served. Dad, you've waited over two decades for this moment so you want to take full advantage of your allotted time. Stand up. Where? You want the "power position" — where all can see you and hear your gift of eloquence. The head table is fine. The stage with the band, or even the center of the room. You want to face everyone in the room.

Stand up, and with your confident voice say, "Ladies and Gentlemen, may I have your attention," or something to that effect. You may have to say this two or three times. One good attention-getter that is guaranteed to get you silence, is the always reliable, "Shhhhhh!" Add some drama by placing your index finger over your mouth when you are "Shhhhhing!" Don't laugh, it works. You want silence. Don't try to talk over people. This procedure takes about 5 seconds (I know, it seems a lot longer). Then introduce the best man. After he delivers his best wishes, Dad, you're back in charge.

Introduce your new son-in-law so he can make his toast. Next, it's the bride's turn, if she so chooses. And then, Dad, your moment has arrived. Go for the gold! If you've done your homework you can get this crowd laughing and crying inside of three minutes. Remember, you're creating an everlasting memory for you, your family, and all the people gathered to listen to you. This is your chance to give everyone a "gift." It is a gift that they will always remember.

Dad, once you've raised your glass and taken a drink, it is then entirely appropriate for the groom's father to offer his toast. Mothers of both the bride and groom should also join the festivities. On this day, ladies, you should also let the banquet hall hear your gift of expression.

The Reply

As is universally the case, the person being toasted does not rise or drink the toast. Saying "Thank you," or a simple, "Here's to you!" is sufficient.

A Toxic Toast

Something to avoid at the wedding reception is what can be referred to as the "blinding glimpse of the obvious" toast by an unconvinced father-in-law:

"We're very happy to see Susan getting married — finally. When I first met Larry, I didn't care for him much. The purple hair and numerous body piercings along with the fact that he didn't have a steady job, sorta bothered me. But he's not that bad. I imagine that Susan could change him —if she wanted, but hey, she seems to like him for what he is. My wife, Gertrude, and I are really sorry Larry's mother couldn't attend — what's her name? It sure would have been nice if his dad would have brought his new trophy wife, but I guess it's just as well. Anyway, where was I? Oh, yeah, that's about all I have for now. Let's have a drink. Was I supposed to propose a toast to these lovely newlyweds?"

With a downbeat message like this, you'll be certain to be remembered — for bringing red faces to some, anger to others, and disappointment to one and all. Three words: don't do it.

CHRISTENING

The Toasters and order of appearance:

1. Godparents
2. Parents
3. Siblings
4. Guests

In most cases the recipient of this toast will be too young to remember the spiritual communication recited on this milestone date. Nonetheless, as we have stated before, the one purpose of any toast is to bring happiness to all who are listening.

ANNIVERSARY

The Toasters and order of appearance:

1. Husband to Wife
2. Wife to Husband
3. Children to Parents
4. Guests

An anniversary provides a time to reflect upon the past, the present, and of course, the future. Anniversaries signal unique opportunities to express your true feelings about the significance of any relationship. While most anniversary toasts would be directed to your spouse or significant other, there are events or achievements that also deserve recognition. What all anniversary toasts have in common is that they should also be a tribute to what is important in life — time well spent with others.

Work

The Toasters and order of appearance:

1. Firm's Spokesperson to Audience
2. Firm's Spokesperson to Employee
3. Fellow Workers
4. Employee to Audience

Just start a new business? Finally get that promotion? Or, is it time to retire? Each and every goal that you reach in your working life calls for eloquence as well. In these toasts the toaster has a wide range of tones to choose from. Humor, sincerity, and growth might represent the backbone of a new business or a promotion. While nostalgia, accomplishments, and cooperation might characterize a salute to a retiring employee.

Fool Yourself

Fool Yourself

It happens to the best and the brightest: Stagefright. Mark Twain, Bob Hope, Ronald Reagan, David Lettermen, Margaret Thatcher, all the great communicators get a little nervous before they go before an audience. Why should you and I be any different? To calm any "nerves" you have before you deliver your toast, here's a great actor's trick: Pick out the one line you know will knock them dead. Focus on this one "hook" line and repeat it over and over again. This focus and repetition will energize you and eradicate any negative thoughts you may have.

Then, fool yourself. The brain and the body can't tell the difference between fear and excitement! So go ahead and fool your brain. Fool your body. How? By telling yourself how much you're ***looking forward to presenting your toast.***

The Value of a Toast

The Value of a Toast

The true worth of any man or woman is not in the value of their possessions, but in the values that guide their lives. Each of us cannot help but make an impact on the lives of others, if we live by a code of strong values. Love, happiness, truth, wisdom, patience, joy, and each of the pages that follow, celebrate rock solid values, virtues, and qualities that are worthy of any toast. Strong values are what make a person great. They can also apply to an organization, a business, or a nation. Strong values are worthy and honorable to lead a life of delight. We honor and pay tribute to those who exemplify and embody such values by raising our glass and making a toast to them.

You might choose one, two or three of these values to build your theme for your toast. These are words that will inspire, motivate, and uplift any occasion. In order to make your toast as unique as you are, expand on these quotations with your own eloquence. What makes your toast unique is the presence of you in its creation. It tells people who you are. In the final analysis, you have only one thing to offer the world that no one else can give: you. You see, we all go for something unique and original — and that's YOU!

Themes

THE EVENT

THE DATE

THE TOAST

BEVERAGE USED

To Achievement

To accomplish anything worthwhile we must dedicate ourselves to the task. Fancy cars, homes, and Swiss watches can be symbols of success and there is nothing wrong with their acquisition. However, if you really want to impress yourself, then a high priority is to become the best you can in the area of your own choosing. Each of us has the potential to become the person that we want to be. Think about what you want to achieve, set goals, and then work at becoming you.

To Achievement

Money buys everything, but love, personality, freedom, immortality, silence, peace.

CARL SANDBURG, POET

When I was a young man I observed that nine out of ten things I did were failures. I didn't want to be a failure, so I did ten times more work.

GEORGE BERNARD SHAW, DRAMATIST

'Tis God gives skill, but not without man's hand: He could not make Antonio Stradivarius' violins without Antonio.

GEORGE ELIOT, NOVELIST

No man, ever became great except through many and great mistakes.

WILLIAM GLADSTONE, STATESMAN

You will be remembered by what you leave behind.

ANONYMOUS

To Achievement

For a man not to achieve the things he has an opportunity to do is such a waste of life. Not for selfishness, but for what you can do for others.

JAKE SIMMONS, JR. OIL BARON

Immortality is not a gift,
Immortality is an achievement;
And only those who strive mightily
Shall possess it.

EDGAR LEE MASTERS, POET

It is a rough road that leads to the heights of achievement.

SENECA, PHILOSOPHER

He who gains a victory over other men is strong, but he who gains a victory over himself is all powerful.

LAO-TZU, PHILOSOPHER

Every great achievement is the result of a flaming heart.

HARRY S. TRUMAN, PRESIDENT

THE EVENT

THE DATE

THE TOAST

BEVERAGE USED

To Character

When I think of Ronald Reagan, I think of a man of character. He is honest, kind, courageous, generous, humorous, spirited, friendly, and filled with integrity. One day, I would like to make a toast to this great President, for he epitomizes this quality. Character is what we do. Our actions tell others quite vividly who we are and what we believe in. Every person has a character, but few are *of* character. There can be no greater compliment than to tell someone that they are a person *of* character.

To Character

Parents can only give good advice or put children on the right paths, but the final forming of a person's character lies in his own hands.

ANNE FRANK, DIARIST

The true test of character is not how much we know how to do, but how we behave when we don't know what to do.

JOHN HOLT, TEACHER

The true test of a man's breeding is how he behaves in a quarrel.

GEORGE BERNARD SHAW, DRAMATIST

Nearly all men can stand adversity, but if you want to test a man's character, give him power.

ABRAHAM LINCOLN, PRESIDENT

It is the character of a brave and resolute person not to be ruffled by adversity and not to desert his post.

CICERO, ROMAN ORATOR

Talent develops in solitude, character in life's torrent.

JOHANN VON GOETHE, PHILOSOPHER

To Character

Character cannot be developed in ease and quiet. Only through experience of trial and suffering can the soul be strengthened, vision cleared, ambition inspired, and success achieved.

HELEN KELLER, AUTHOR, LECTURER

When the character of a man is not clear to you, look at his friends.

JAPANESE PROVERB

Good character consists of two qualities: empathy, meaning regard for the needs, rights, and feelings of others; and self-control, meaning the ability to act with reference to the more distant consequences of current behavior.

JAMES WILSON, UCLA PROFESSOR

Firmness of purpose is one of the most necessary sinews of character, and one of the best instruments of success.

PHILIP CHESTERFIELD, DIPLOMAT

Focus on your character and success will come naturally.

CONFUCIUS, PHILOSOPHER

The Event

The Date

The Toast

Beverage Used

To Commitment

Successful people in all walks of life can be counted on. They are dependable. They are like a Rolex watch: reliable. Successful individuals show their commitment by doing just what they say they will do. To show that you are committed, your words must be backed by actions. If you make a mistake, admit it. People think a lot more of you and are forgiving when you admit your mistake. Finally, your trust level soars when you display commitment. Trust in our personal and professional life is the coin of the realm.

To Commitment

In all circumstances, what matters most is whether or not you can make a commitment.

STEVE DEYO, WRITER

If you're going to do something, you have to be committed and make the sacrifices it demands.

NOLAN RYAN, BASEBALL GREAT

Little happens in a relationship until the individuals learn to trust each other.

DAVID JOHNSON, COUNSELOR

It is not who is right, but what is right.

ANONYMOUS

If someone listens, or stretches out a hand, or whispers a word of encouragement, or attempts to understand a lonely person, extraordinary things can happen.

LORETTA GIRZARTIS, WRITER

To Commitment

In this world, sometimes we have to give 100% to something that we are 51% sure of.

Albert Camus, writer

Men must be decided on what they will not do, and then they are able to act with vigor in what they ought to do.

Mencius, philosopher

Do your duty, and leave the rest to heaven.

Pierre Corneille, dramatist

Duty is the most sublime word in our language. Do your duty in all things. You should never wish to do less.

Robert E. Lee, general

The woods are lovely, dark, and deep.
But I have promises to keep,
And miles to go before I sleep
And miles to go before I sleep.

Robert Frost, poet

THE EVENT

THE DATE

THE TOAST

BEVERAGE USED

To Courage

To be brave is to be good. To be good is to have courage to face the crises, catastrophes, and conflicts that come your way. Show me a person who deals with a life crisis with humor, honor, and dignity and I will show you a person with courage. A person of courage can never eliminate the risks, the pains, the unknown. Instead, they work their way through each difficulty. A courageous person is someone who loves themself enough to not give in to self-doubt, rejection, or fear. They march forward and do what ought to be done.

To Courage

Courage is fear holding on a minute longer.

GEORGE PATTON, GENERAL

Life shrinks or expands according to one's courage.

ANAIS NIN, WRITER

Courage is not simply one of the virtues, but the form of every virtue at the testing point.

C. S. LEWIS, LITERARY SCHOLAR

Courage is not a value or virtue among other personal values like love or fidelity. It is the foundation that underlies and gives reality to all other virtues and personal values.

ROLLO MAY, PSYCHOLOGIST

Cowards die many times before their deaths, the valiant never taste death but once.

WILLIAM SHAKESPEARE, DRAMATIST

To Courage

The greatest test of courage is to bear defeat without losing heart.

ROBERT G. INGERSOLL, ORATOR

Life is mostly froth and bubble,
Two things stand like stone,
Kindness in another's trouble,
Courage in your own.

ADAM LINDSAY GORDON, POET

Keep fighting. The health, happiness, and success of every person depends upon a fighting spirit.

GEORGE AKIN, WRITER

Cultivate a measure of equanimity so as to bear success with humility, the affection of your friends without pride, and be ready when the day of sorrow and grief come, so as to meet that day with courage befitting a man.

SIR WILLIAM OSLER, PHYSICIAN

Courage is the price that life exacts for granting peace.

AMELIA EARHART, AVIATOR

The Event

The Date

The Toast

Beverage Used

To Endurance

All of us have lofty dreams, ideas, and goals. Those who never, never give up in their quest deserve all honors. They have what it takes to endure the pain, the hardship, the adversity, the pressure, the humiliation, and the discouragement that often accompany such pursuits. Such people live by the Latin phrase, "Fortitudine vincimus" — by endurance, we conquer. Their pervading characteristic? They are purposeful.

To Endurance

Smooth seas do not make for skillful sailors.

AFRICAN PROVERB

The art of life is to know how to enjoy a little and to endure much.

WILLIAM HAZLITT, ESSAYIST

The race doesn't belong to the swift and the brave, but to he who endures until the end.

ARMSTRONG WILLIAMS, EDUCATOR

Always go forward and never turn back.

JUNIPERO SERRA, FRANCISCAN FRIAR

Never let a little adversity stand in your way from reaching your goal. It is the ability to endure pain, hardship, and suffering that sweetens success.

STEVE DEYO, WRITER

Let me tell you the secret that has led me to my goal. My strength lies solely in my tenacity.

LOUIS PASTEUR, SCIENTIST

To Endurance

Great works are performed not by strength, but by perseverance.

SAMUEL JOHNSON, AUTHOR

Heroism, the Caucasian mountaineers say, is endurance for one moment more.

GEORGE KENNAN, POLITICAL ANALYST

The true test of any man or woman is their ability to endure all difficulties in order to reach their goal.

ANONYMOUS

It is not the mountain we conquer, but ourselves.

SIR EDMUND HILLARY, ADVENTURER

To every obstacle oppose patience, perseverance, and soothing language.

THOMAS JEFFERSON, PRESIDENT

A warrior must endure physical pain, hunger, and thirst without complaint. A warrior must handle his personal life with reserve, consideration, and dignity.

SECOND VIRTUE OF A SIOUX WARRIOR

THE EVENT

THE DATE

THE TOAST

BEVERAGE USED

To Enthusiasm

The word enthusiasm is a combination of the Greek word "theos," meaning God, and the French word, "en," which means to be inspired. Therefore, if you are enthusiastic, you are being inspired by God. From beginning to end, your life is a true miracle. If you wish to be enthusiastic, all you have to do is act enthusiastic. Your belief in the success of any worthwhile project is determined by your level of enthusiasm. Everything goes better with a lot of enthusiasm placed in the mixture.

To Enthusiasm

Let your enthusiasm radiate in your voice, your actions, your facial expressions, your personality, the words you use, and the thoughts you think! Nothing great was ever achieved without enthusiasm.

RALPH WALDO EMERSON, ESSAYIST

The secret of genius is to carry the spirit of the child into old age, which means never losing your enthusiasm.

ALDOUS HUXLEY, NOVELIST

Apathy can only be overcome by enthusiasm.

ARNOLD TOYNBEE, PHILOSOPHER

Me? I loved to hit.

BABE RUTH, BASEBALL GREAT

All we need to be happy is something to be enthusiastic about.

CHARLES KINGSLEY, ESSAYIST

Success is the ability to go from failure to failure with no loss of enthusiasm.

WINSTON CHURCHILL, STATESMAN

To Enthusiasm

I have no special talents. I am only passionately curious.

ALBERT EINSTEIN, PHYSICIST

A weak spirit does more harm than a weak body.

BALTASAR GRACIAN, JESUIT PRIEST

You have within you the power to live your dreams, if only you will control your thoughts.

WALLY AMOS, ENTREPRENEUR

Enthusiasm, like measles, mumps, and the common cold, is highly contagious.

EMORY WARD, WRITER

Enthusiasm reflects confidence, spreads good cheer, raises morale, inspires associates, arouses loyalty and laughs at adversity...it is beyond price.

ALLEN COX, BUSINESS CONSULTANT

Dancing eyes, sparkling words, and neopolitan gestures signal enthusiasm.

STEVE DEYO, WRITER

THE EVENT

THE DATE

THE TOAST

BEVERAGE USED

To Family

Life's greatest happinesses are family happinesses. Wonderful moments with your family do not last, they pass. No moment lasts forever. Be playful with your spouse. Be playful with your children. Take those summer vacations to national parks, the beach, or the mountains. There is nothing more satisfying than a home filled with positive emotions that uplift each person in the family. Laughing, playing, and enjoying such life experiences will serve you well when times of sadness, sorrow, or somber come.

To Family

Shared joy is double joy, and shared sorrow is half sorrow.

SWEDISH PROVERB.

There are two lasting bequests we can give our children. One is roots. The other is wings.

HODDING CARTER, JR. JOURNALIST

The only true gift is a portion of thyself.

RALPH WALDO EMERSON, ESSAYIST

Whoever you are, there's someone who thinks perfect. There is someone who would miss you if you were gone. There is a place that you alone can fill.

JACOB BRAUDE, WRITER

The greatest gift you can give another is the purity of your attention.

RICHARD MOSS, NOVELIST

The greatest thing in family life is to take a hint when a hint is intended — and not to take a hint when a hint isn't intended.

ROBERT FROST, POET

To Family

The root of the kingdom is in the state. The root of the state is in the family. The root of the family is in the person of its head.

MENCIUS, PHILOSOPHER

May the gods grant you all the things which your heart desires, and may they give you a husband and a home and gracious concord, for there is nothing greater than this — when a husband and wife keep a household in oneness of mind, a great woe to their enemies and joy to their friends, and win renown.

HOMER, GREEK WRITER

We're here to enjoy ourselves and to play . Playing keeps us young at heart and helps our relationships thrive. To play is to live life to its fullest.

DAVID KESSLER, MEDICAL RESEARCHER

Give your children love, guidance, instruction, and discipline and your job as a parent will be complete.

ANONYMOUS

THE EVENT

THE DATE

THE TOAST

BEVERAGE USED

To Friendship

You can make wine without grapes, but you cannot make wine without yeast. Friends are to life as yeast is to wine. Without true friends life is like the Atacama Desert — barren, desolate, and empty. Cultivate the art of friendship. It is a true measure of any man or woman to say that they have many friends. While it may sound trite, we are all judged by the friends we keep, so make sure you have only the best.

To Friendship

A friend is all things and friendship has the three qualities of anything good: unity; goodness; and truth. Life without friends is a wasteland.

BALTASAR GRACIAN, JESUIT PRIEST

I've traveled many a highway
I've walked many a mile
Here's to the people who made my day
To the people who waved and smiled.

TOM T. HALL, SINGER, SONG WRITER

Friends are life's greatest treasure.

C.M. RUSSELL, ARTIST, SCULPTOR

A friend is someone who sees through you and still enjoys the view.

WILMA ASKINAS, WRITER

A faithful friend is the medicine of life.

THE HOLY BIBLE: ECCLESIASTES

To Friendship

Friendship is the pleasing game of interchanging praise.

Oliver Wendell Holmes, poet

Friendship is the wine of life.

James Boswell, writer

A friend loveth at all times, and a brother is born for adversity.

The Holy Bible: Proverbs 17:17

A friend may well be reckoned the masterpiece of nature.

Ralph Waldo Emerson, essayist

I am wealthy in my friends.

William Shakespeare, dramatist

A true friend is the person who steps in when the whole world steps out.

Anonymous

THE EVENT

THE DATE

THE TOAST

BEVERAGE USED

To Happiness

Most of us would like to live "happily ever after." Yet, at some point, we realize that a fairy tale life is not only unreachable, but also fairly boring. Life is a mortal paradox. It is meant to be beautiful at times and less than beautiful at others. It is gloriously comic some days and tragic on other days. It is chaotic and it is tranquil. Being happy means accepting this paradox and realizing that happiness is the result of being your best at all times.

To Happiness

There is only one happiness in life, to love and to be loved.

George Sand, novelist

The supreme happiness of life is the conviction that we are loved.

Victor Hugo, writer

Values, not pleasures, are what bring true happiness, and everybody has the potential to live in accordance with their values.

John Stuart Mill, philosopher

It is not easy to find happiness in ourselves and it is not possible to find it elsewhere.

Agnes Repplier, writer

Happiness does not depend on outward things, but on the way we see them.

Leo Tolstoy. Novelist

Happiness is good health and a bad memory.

Ingrid Bergman, actress

To Happiness

The secret to happiness is freedom and the secret of freedom is a brave heart.

Thucydides, Athenian historian

True happiness arises in the first place from the enjoyment of oneself.

Joseph Addison, poet

The goal of every person is quite simple: to die happy.

Albert Camus, writer

There is no duty we so much underrate as that of being happy.

Robert Louis Stevenson, novelist

Let everyone you meet be happier having met you, for having spoken to you.

Edgar Cayce, Psychic Reader

To find true happiness: Reminisce.

Giacomo Casanova, romanticist

THE EVENT

THE DATE

THE TOAST

BEVERAGE USED

To Humor

Humor serves as a shock absorber to the adversity we sometimes encounter. All of us experience problems, failures, and disappointments during this journey and humor absorbs their impact. Humor reminds us that we are finite, fallible, and frequently foolish. It is also the best way to keep the "customers" wide awake during your toast.

To Humor

No mind is thoroughly well organized that is deficient in a sense of humor.

SAMUEL TAYLOR COLERIDGE, POET

Only if we are secure in our beliefs can we see the comical side of the universe.

FLANNERY O'CONNOR, WRITER

A keen sense of humor helps us to overlook the unbecoming, understand the unconventional, tolerate the unpleasant, overcome the unexpected and outlast the unbearable.

BILLY GRAHAM, EVANGELIST

Humor is a prelude to faith and laughter is the beginning of prayer.

REINHOLD NIEBUHR, THEOLOGIAN

If you wish to glimpse inside a human soul and get to know a man, don't bother analyzing his ways of being silent, of talking, weeping, or seeing how he is moved by noble ideas; you'll get better results if you just watch him laugh. If he laughs well, he's a good man.

FYODER DOSTOYEVSKI, NOVELIST

To Humor

If you don't have a sense of humor, you probably don't have any sense at all.

GRANDMA MACDONALD, PHILOSOPHER

Life is too confusing and too grim to be taken seriously — laughter sometimes is the only way out.

PHILIP ROTH, NOVELIST

Everything human is pathetic. The secret source of humor itself is not joy, but sorrow. There is no humor in heaven.

MARK TWAIN, HUMORIST

A joyful heart is good medicine, but a broken spirit dries up the bones.

THE HOLY BIBLE: PROVERBS, 17:22

Happy are the hard-boiled, for they never let life hurt them.

J.B. PHILLIPS, WRITER

Laughter is healthy. If you suppress laughter it goes back down to your hips. Imagine how painful it would be if it settled in your colon.

ANONYMOUS

The Event

The Date

The Toast

Beverage Used

To Joy

Ask yourself, "What gives me joy?" Then, periodically, do those things that give you joy. Joy must be part of your life plan. When we do the things that give us joy, our family, friends, and everyone we encounter sees it in our eyes and on our face. Real joy is not a lack of difficulty in our life, but knowledge that life is a fragile bargain to be celebrated. By experiencing as many joyful moments as you can, you accomplish two goals: 1) you make yourself happy; and 2) you make this a better world because joy is contagious.

To Joy

Joy and openness come from our own contented heart.

BUDDHA, SPIRITUAL LEADER

Grief can take care of itself, but to get the full value of joy, you must have somebody to share it with.

MARK TWAIN, AUTHOR

See golden days, fruitful of golden deeds, with joy and love triumphing.

JOHN MILTON, DRAMATIST

Man was made for joy and woe,
And when this we rightly know
Through the world we safely go.

WILLIAM BLAKE, POET

The most visible joy can only reveal itself to us when we've transformed it, within.

RAINER MARIA RILKE, POET

Joy always comes after pain.

GUILLAUME APOLLINAIRE, POET

To Joy

Follow your bliss.

Joseph Campbell, scholar

Joy is prayer, joy is strength, joy is love. Joy is a net of love by which you can catch souls.

Mother Teresa, Catholic nun

Joy is not in things, it is in us.

Richard Wagner, composer

I drink to the general joy of the whole table.

William Shakespeare, dramatist

Make it your business to learn how to feel joy.

Seneca, Roman philosopher

Joy is the emotional expression of the courageous, Yes! to one's true self.

Anonymous

THE EVENT

THE DATE

THE TOAST

BEVERAGE USED

To Life

How many of us really appreciate the greatest gift given to us — Life. It has been said that life is God's gift to you. What you and I do during our life is our gift to Him . Life is a celebration and how we spend our days is a reflection of who we are. Marvel at each moment. Delight in each day. And savor each sunset. The fiesta of life awaits.

To Life

Life is either a daring adventure, or it is nothing.

HELEN KELLER, AUTHOR, LECTURER

To do the useful thing, to say the courageous thing, to contemplate the beautiful thing: that is enough for one man's life.

T.S. ELIOT, POET, DRAMATIST

It is good to have an end to journey towards, but it is the journey that matters in the end.

URSULA LEGUIN, NOVELIST

I have found that if you love life, life will love you back.

ARTHUR RUBINSTEIN, PIANIST

Never confuse a single defeat with a final defeat.

F. SCOTT FITZGERALD, NOVELIST

People break hearts and time mends them. Time breaks spirits and people mend them. All broken spirits need to be exposed repeatedly to the light of as many warm personalities as possible.

MARILYN VOS SAVANT, WRITER

To Life

The purpose of life is to matter, to be productive, to have it make some difference that you have lived at all.

LEO ROSTEN, PHILOSOPHER

He who knows he has enough is rich.

TAO TE CHING, PHILOSOPHER

Regret for the things we've done can be tempered with time; it is regret for the things we did not do, that is inconsolable.

SIDNEY J. HARRIS, WRITER

There are three chapters in our autobiography: one chapter tells of our deeds; one chapter of our words; and a final chapter of our art.

STEVE DEYO, WRITER

The only things one never regrets are ones mistakes.

OSCAR WILDE, PLAYWRIGHT

THE EVENT

THE DATE

THE TOAST

BEVERAGE USED

To Love

Throughout the ages, philosophers have said: to discover the meaning of love we must first love ourselves. We cannot truly love another, if we do not love ourselves first. Someone to love in our life is paramount for a meaningful existence and makes each day a joy. Without love, life is an empty vessel. Show the ones you love how much you care for them by giving them your time, attention, and support in good times, bad times, and in-between times.

To Love

Your name, my love, will always be written on the inside of my heart.

Steve Deyo, Writer

You are the delight of my life. Your kindness, courtesy, respect, and spirit have filled my days with love.

Anonymous

I love thee with the breath, smiles, tears, of all my life! And if God choose, I shall but love thee better after death.

Elizabeth Barrett Browning, Poet

You have deserved his commendation, true applause and love.

William Shakespeare, Writer

The man or woman you really love will never grow old to you. Through the wrinkles of time, through the bowed frame of years, you will always see and feel the warm heart of your eternal love.

Alfred A. Montpert, Writer

To Love

Whatever you do...love those who love you.

VOLTAIRE, WRITER

The meeting of two personalities is like the contact of two chemical substances; if there is a reaction, both are transformed.

CARL GUSTAV JUNG, PSYCHIATRIST

To love somebody is not just a strong feeling, it is a decision, it is a judgement, it is a promise. If love were only a feeling, there would be no basis for the promise to love each other forever. A feeling comes and it may go.

ERIC FROMM, PSYCHIATRIST

We love the things we love for what we are.

ROBERT FROST, POET

THE EVENT

THE DATE

THE TOAST

BEVERAGE USED

To Man/Woman

Interesting men and women are like the leaves of autumn: colorful, unique, and fun to be around. Books are written about men and women who are not conformists. These men and women are not afraid to dare, not afraid to risk, and not afraid to follow their passion. These men and women checked their fears at the front door of society's conforming ways and blazed their own trail. Wanted: Men and Women who can do and dare.

To Man/Woman

To a brave man, good luck and bad luck are like the right and left hand. They use both.

St. Catherine of Siena, Dominican Tertiary

I love the man in trouble who can smile and gather strength from distress and grow brave by reflection.

Thomas Paine, patriot

As many languages as he has, as many friends, as many arts and trades, so many times is he a man.

Ralph Waldo Emerson, essayist

What you are must always displease you in order for you to attain that which you are not.

St. Augustine, archbishop of Canterbury

A life spent making mistakes is not only more honorable, but more useful, than a life doing nothing.

George Bernard Shaw, dramatist

To Man/Woman

Chiefly, the mold of a man's future is in his own hands.

Sir Francis Bacon, Essayist

You can measure a man by the amount of opposition it takes to discourage them.

Robert Savage, Writer, Inventor

A musician must make music, an artist must paint, a poet must write, if he is to be at peace with himself. What a man can be, he must be.

Abraham Maslow, Psychologist

Anyone who takes himself too seriously always runs the risk of looking ridiculous; anyone who can consistently laugh at himself does not.

Vaclav Havel, Czech President

First, say to yourself what you would be; and then do what you have to do.

Epictetus, Greek Philosopher

There is no better measure of a person than what he does when he is free to choose.

Wilma Askinas, Writer

THE EVENT

THE DATE

THE TOAST

BEVERAGE USED

To Marriage

You want a great marriage? Is there a secret formula? Some secret sauce? Well, to give yourself a proprietary advantage you might listen to what the experts say: 1) Let him/her nag; 2) never marry a person you wouldn't trust to sign your checks; 3) stay out of debt (other than a home mortgage); 4) touch, kiss, and hold hands; 5) share your day and ask him/her about his/hers; 6) think kindness, courtesy, and respect in all communication; 7) show some spirit! A great marriage happens when two imperfect people learn to enjoy their differences.

To Marriage

The great question which I have never been able to answer is, "What does a woman want?"

SIGMUND FREUD, PSYCHIATRIST

Being a husband is just like any other job: it's much easier if you like your boss.

ANONYMOUS

It's a funny thing that when a man hasn't anything on earth to worry about, he goes off and gets married.

ROBERT FROST, POET

Before you marry, ask yourself five questions: Does this person have character? Are they kind, considerate, respectful and filled with spirit? If the answers are all yes, then, get thee to a jewelry store.

STEVE DEYO, WRITER

Marriage: A community consisting of a master, a mistress, and two slaves, making in all, two.

AMBROSE BIERCE, SATIRIST

To Marriage

There is no more lovely, friendly and charming relationship, communion or company, than a good marriage.

Martin Luther, theologian

Keep your eyes wide open before marriage, half shut afterwards.

Benjamin Franklin, printer

The heart of marriage is memories.

Bill Cosby, comedian

Marriage has many pains, but celibacy has no pleasures.

Samuel Johnson, poet

A deaf husband and a blind wife are always a happy couple.

16th century proverb

The value of a marriage is not that adults produce children, but that children produce adults.

Peter DeVries, novelist

THE EVENT

THE DATE

THE TOAST

BEVERAGE USED

To Obstacles

One of the great challenges you and I face whenever we begin a new stage of life, a new project, or a new situation is the ability to overcome the obstacles in our path. Obstacles can be real or imagined, and they block our way. Actually, they are just the price of admission to any new adventure. A better term for obstacles should be confidence builders.

To Obstacles

I have learned that success is to be measured not so much by the position that one has reached in life, as by the obstacles which he has overcome while trying to succeed.

Booker T. Washington, social reformer

The very greatest things, great thoughts, discoveries, inventions, have been nurtured in hardship, often pondered over in sorrow, at length established with great difficulty.

Samuel Smiles, writer

Even when confronted with a hopeless situation, you still have a chance to make life meaningful. . . in turning personal tragedy into a triumph or by transforming your predicament to an accomplishment.

Viktor Frankl, psychiatrist

No one can become strong without struggle with adversity, resistance, and problems. Struggle makes us strong, and in the process of over coming, we achieve happiness. We learn thereby, how, despite everything, life can be a joyous adventure.

Anonymous

To Obstacles

To every obstacle, oppose patience, perseverance, and soothing language.

THOMAS JEFFERSON, PRESIDENT

I am not surprised at what men suffer, but I am surprised at what men miss.

JOHN RUSKIN, WRITER

Those things that hurt, instruct.

BENJAMIN FRANKLIN, PRINTER

There is less to this than meets the eye.

TALLULAH BANKHEAD, ACTOR

Don't ever let your problems become an excuse.

ANONYMOUS

Problems are the cutting edge that distinguishes between success and failure. Problems call forth our courage and our wisdom; indeed, they create courage and wisdom.

SCOTT PECK, PSYCHIATRIST

THE EVENT

THE DATE

THE TOAST

BEVERAGE USED

To Optimism

Rejection, frustration, and difficulties can often be a daily diet. Therefore, we must think optimistically. Optimism prolongs life and powers the body's immune system. Optimism is "eyes wide open" to endless possibilities. Optimism is a tool to reach your goals and achieve your purpose.

To Optimism

Twixt the optimist and pessimist
The difference is droll:
The optimist sees the doughnut
But the pessimist sees the hole.

McLandburg Wilson, writer

The optimist proclaims that we live in the best of all possible worlds; and the pessimist fears that this is true.

James Branch Cabell, novelist

A weak faith is weakened by predicaments and catastrophes; whereas a strong faith is strengthened by them.

Viktor Frankl, psychiatrist

I am seeking; I am striving; I am in it with all my heart.

Vincent van Gogh, artist

Your biggest competitor is your own view of the your future.

Watts Wacker, consultant

To Optimism

Optimism is a choice, and one of the most powerful we can make.

Ronald Reagan, President

A pessimist sees the difficulty in every opportunity; an optimist sees the opportunity in every difficulty.

Winston Churchill, Prime Minister

If I was not optimistic, I would not be an architect.

Jacobus Oud, Architect

An optimist is a person who sees a green light everywhere, while a pessimist sees only the red light. The truly wise person is color blind.

Albert Schweitzer, medical missionary

Anticipate good outcomes, do your best, leave it to God, and believe all will come out right.

Norman Vincent Peale, minister

THE EVENT

THE DATE

THE TOAST

BEVERAGE USED

To Patience

Leo Tolstoy, the Russian novelist, said, "time and patience are the strongest of warriors." Still, in the wireless world of the 21st century we seldom place patience in everyday practice. We want it now. We can't wait. Tomorrow is too late. Patience is the emotional discipline to do our duty, stay the course, and keep working toward our goal despite our changing moods. Patience predicts achievement, life fulfillment, and contribution. During periods of maximum stress when you're fighting one of life's battles, make sure you have patience by your side.

To Patience

The strongest of all warriors are these two: Time and Patience.

Leo Tolstoy, novelist

Patience is the most necessary requirement for business.

Lord Chesterfield, statesman

How poor are they that have not patience. What wound did ever heal but by degrees?

William Shakespeare, dramatist

Patience is the best remedy for every trouble.

Titus Plautus, dramatist

Genius is nothing but a greater aptitude for patience.

George de Buffon, naturalist

Be patient with yourself. After all, you're life is a work in progress.

Anonymous

Possess your soul with patience. Beware the fury of a patient man.

John Dryden, poet, dramatist

To Patience

Often, to lose patience is to lose the battle.

MAHATMA GANDHI, SPIRITUAL LEADER

Patience, faith, and understanding are qualities of universal importance.

STEVE DEYO, WRITER

Keep strong, if possible. In any case, keep cool. Have unlimited patience. Never corner an opponent, and always assist him to save face. Put yourself in his shoes — so as to see things through his eyes. Avoid self-righteousness like the devil — nothing so self-blinding.

BASIL LIDDELL HART, STATESMAN

Ever since man began to till the soil and learned not to eat the seed grain, but to plant it and wait for the harvest, the postponement of gratification has been the basis of a higher standard of living and civilization.

S. I. HAYAKAWA, SCHOLAR

Always hear the other side.

LATIN PROVERB

THE EVENT

THE DATE

THE TOAST

BEVERAGE USED

To Persistence

Stay the course. Never give up. Do not waver. This is what it means to have persistence. It has been said that the major factor in any accomplishment is the ability to persist when all seems lost. Statistics tell us that most sales are closed after at least five "No's." Excellence in any profession, sport, or activity requires persistence.

To Persistence

To strive, to seek, to find, and not to yield.

Alfred Lord Tennyson, poet

Obstacles cannot crush me. Every obstacle yields to stern resolve. He who is fixed to a star does not change his mind.

Leonardo da Vinci, painter, sculptor

Other people give up. I just don't give up. That's how to succeed.

Harrison Ford, actor

Persistence is what makes the impossible, possible, the possible likely, and the likely, definite.

Robert Half, consultant

The block of granite which was an obstacle in the path of the weak, becomes a stepping stone in the path of the strong.

Thomas Carlyle, essayist

To Persistence

If you falter in times of trouble, how small is your strength!

The Holy Bible: Proverbs 24:10

The habit of persistence is the habit of victory.

Albert Einstein, physicist

You would be surprised how many people quit when faced with obstacles. As every good salesman knows, everything may not be possible today, but sooner or later, it is possible.

Earl Graves, publisher

Success depends on staying power. The reason for failure in most cases is a lack of determination.

Jim Murray, sportswriter

In business, sometimes prospects may seem darkest when really they are on the turn. A little more persistence, a little more effort, and what seemed hopeless, may turn to glorious success.

Elbert Hubbard, Editor

THE EVENT

THE DATE

THE TOAST

BEVERAGE USED

To Respect

Respect is the alpha and the omega of healthy relationships. We achieve respect by behaving respectably. A lack of respect for ourselves, others, and things is a recipe for destructive behavior. Respect yourself. Respect others. And be Responsible for your actions are the three R's of a meaningful life. To say that we respect someone or something is to award a badge of distinction and dignity.

To Respect

The four commandments from the Great Spirit are: 1) respect for Mother Earth; 2) respect for the Great Spirit; 3) respect for your fellow man; and 4) respect for individual freedom (provided that individual freedom does not threaten the people, the tribe, or Mother Earth).

Ed McGaa, Oglala Sioux

You have too much respect upon the world: They lose it that do not buy it with much care.

William Shakespeare, dramatist

If you want to be respected by others, the great thing is to respect yourself.

Fyodor Dostoyevsky, novelist

A man's real life is that accorded to him in the thoughts of other men by reason of respect for natural love.

Joseph Conrad, novelist

To Respect

I believe that I should treat the fan in the bleachers the same way I would treat the President — with respect.

NOLAN RYAN, BASEBALL GREAT

What we obtain too cheap, we esteem too lightly; 'tis dearness only that gives everything its value.

THOMAS PAINE, PATRIOT

So much is a man worth as he esteems himself.

FRANCOIS RABELAIS, AUTHOR

Mine honor is my life; both grow in one;
Take honor from me, and my life is done.

WILLIAM SHAKESPEARE, DRAMATIST

Never esteem men on account of their riches or their station. Respect goodness; find it where you may.

WILLIAM COBBETT, JOURNALIST

THE EVENT

THE DATE

THE TOAST

BEVERAGE USED

To Success

How do you measure success? Is it money? Material possessions? The list can be as long as the Mississippi River, for each of us has our own specific definition. Still, most successful individuals are those who learn to be humble, tolerant, and kind. Those who fail are bitter, insensitive, and unkind.

To Success

To accomplish great things, we must not only act, but also dream, not only plan, but also believe.

ANATOLE FRANCE, WRITER

Do what you love, give it back in the form of service and you will succeed and you will triumph.

OPRAH WINFREY, TALK SHOW HOST

Real success is finding your life's work in the work you love.

DAVID MCCULLOUGH, HISTORIAN

Success has a very simple formula: do your best and people may like it.

SAM EWING, WRITER

A somebody was once a nobody who wanted to and did.

ANONYMOUS

Success is the satisfaction of feeling that one is realizing one's ideal.

ANNA PAVLOVA, BALLET DANCER

To Success

Success is to be measured not so much by the position that one has reached in life as, as by the obstacles he has overcome trying to succeed.

BOOKER T. WASHINGTON, EDUCATOR

Measure wealth not by the things you have, but by the things you have for which you would not take money.

ANONYMOUS

The highest reward for a man's toil is not what he gets for it, but what he becomes by it.

JOHN RUSKIN, SOCIAL THEORIST

Success isn't economic. If you're doing what you like with your life, that's success — personal success.

RAUL JULIA, ACTOR

True success is to honor your calling. You must have the courage to follow your passion.

JAMES HILLMAN, EDUCATOR

Try first to be a man of value; then success will follow.

ALBERT EINSTEIN, PHYSICIST

THE EVENT

THE DATE

THE TOAST

BEVERAGE USED

To Talent

From the day we enter the world we possess certain talents. The challenge of our life is to identify our talents and use them to make this a better world. Far too many of us hide our talents under a peach basket. God gave you these talents for a reason. Put your talents to the test and display them for all to see. Do this, and you will be pleased and so will He. It is never too late in the day to show your talents: Michelangelo was 71 when he became supervisor at the Sistine Chapel; Grandma Moses was also 71 when she painted her first painting; Pablo Casals performed at the White House at the age of 85.

To Talent

The greatest good you can do for another is not to show your riches, but to reveal to them their own.

BENJAMIN DISRAELI, PRIME MINISTER

Talents are common; everyone has them. But rare is the courage to follow our talents where they lead.

ANONYMOUS

It's never too late to be what we might have been.

GEORGE ELIOT, NOVELIST

Mediocrity knows nothing higher than itself, but talent instantly recognizes genius.

SIR ARTHUR CONAN DOYLE, NOVELIST

What you love to do is what you are gifted at.

BARBARA SHER, AUTHOR, LECTURER

Do few things, but do them well.

SIR FRANCIS BACON, ESSAYIST

To Talent

Use what talents you possess; the woods would be very silent if no birds sang except those that sang best.

HENRY VAN DYKE, CLERGYMAN

Hide not your talents,
They for use were made,
What's a sundial in the shade?

BENJAMIN FRANKLIN, PRINTER

If a man has a talent and cannot use it, he has failed. If he has a talent and uses only half of it, he has partly failed. If he has a talent and learns somehow to use the whole of it, he has gloriously succeeded, and won a satisfaction and a triumph few men ever know

THOMAS WOLFE, DRAMATIST

Never have I thought that I was the happy possessor of "talent;" my sole concern has been to save myself by work and faith.

JEAN PAUL SARTRE, WRITER, PHILOSOPHER

THE EVENT

THE DATE

THE TOAST

BEVERAGE USED

To Thought

A great thinker must not surrender to his moods. If someone has been unkind to you, do not allow the unkindness to affect your next conversation. Good events can turn out to be bad events and bad events can turn out to be good events. It is your thinking that colors your perception on the palette of your life.

To Thought

Half of our mistakes in life arise from feeling, when we ought to think and thinking when we ought to feel.

JOHN COLLINS, LECTURER

Human learning has three main parts...history, based on memory, poetry based on the imagination, and philosophy based on reason.

SIR FRANCIS BACON, ESSAYIST

No one can build his security upon the nobleness of another person.

WILLA CATHER, NOVELIST, WRITER

This moment contains all the possibilities for happiness and love. Do not lose these possibilities in expectations of what the future may hold.

E. KUBLER-ROSS, MEDICAL RESEARCHER

Style is the dress of thoughts.

LORD CHESTERFIELD, STATESMAN

To Thought

In this world, second thoughts, it seems, are best.

EURIPIDES, DRAMATIST

They are never alone that are accompanied with noble thoughts.

SIR PHILLIP SIDNEY, POET

All thoughts, all passions, all delights,
Whatever stirs this mortal frame,
All are ministers of love,
And feed his sacred flame.

SAMUEL TAYLOR COLERIDGE, POET

People should be beautiful in every way- in their faces, in the way they dress, in their thoughts and in their innermost selves.

ANTON CHEKHOV, DRAMATIST

Great thoughts come from the heart.

LUC DE CLAPIERS, ESSAYIST

THE EVENT

THE DATE

THE TOAST

BEVERAGE USED

To Uniqueness

Being unique is both a spiritual and an emotional requirement. It's who you are. Do not imitate anyone. Be you. We waste our time when we try to conform to others. To discover and express our own uniqueness must be everyone's supreme goal. We must use the gifts that God gave us and develop them to our highest potential.

To Uniqueness

Every man and woman is put on this earth to do something unique, and if they don't, then it shan't get done. Have faith in whatever you do.

DR. BENJAMIN MAYS, EDUCATOR

While an original is always hard to find, he is easy to recognize.

JOHN MASON, WRITER

This above all: To thine own self be true, and it must follow, as night the day, thou canst not be false to any man.

WILLIAM SHAKESPEARE, DRAMATIST

A man's self is the sum total of all that he can call his, not only his body and his psychic powers, but his clothes and his house, his wife and children, his ancestors and friends, his reputation and works, his lands and horses, and yacht and bank account. All these things give him the same emotions. If they wax and prosper, he feels triumphant; if they dwindle and die away, he feels cast down.

WILLIAM JAMES, PSYCHOLOGIST

To Uniqueness

Individuality of expression is the beginning and end of all art.

JOHANN VON GOETHE, PHILOSOPHER

In modern society, the opposite of courage isn't cowardice; it is conformity.

ROLLO MAY, PSYCHOLOGIST

A lotta cats copy the Mona Lisa. But people still line up to see the original.

LOUIS ARMSTRONG, TRUMPETER

A thought is often original, though you may have uttered it a hundred times.

OLIVER WENDELL HOLMES, POET

She is as unique as the sonatas of Mozart.

ARTUR SCHNABEL, PIANIST

Everybody goes for something unique.

BALTASAR GRACIAN, JESUIT PRIEST

THE EVENT

THE DATE

THE TOAST

BEVERAGE USED

To Wisdom

"We are all ignorant...just on different subjects," were words of cowboy wisdom from humorist, Will Rogers. Most of us may never reach "guru status" in either our personal or professional lives. That's okay. However, we can all be wise if we: 1) pay attention to the world around us; 2) behave in a kind manner toward others; and 3) act critically in any given situation. While each can be difficult, wisdom comes from excellence in all three. It is a tall order. Many are called and few are chosen.

To Wisdom

By three methods we learn wisdom: first, by reflection, which is noblest; second, by imitation, which is easiest; and third, by experience, which is bittersweet.

CONFUSCIUS, PHILOSOPHER

To acquire knowledge one must study, to acquire wisdom one must observe.

MARILYN VOS SAVANT, WRITER

A man's errors are portals to discovery.

JAMES JOYCE, NOVELIST

The art of being wise is the art of knowing what to overlook.

WILLIAM JAMES, PSYCHOLOGIST

He who knows much about others may be learned, but he who understands himself is far more intelligent. They who control others may be powerful, but those who master themselves are mightier still.

LAO-TZU, PHILOSOPHER

The salt of bitterness can be transformed into the salt of wisdom.

CARL JUNG, PSYCHIATRIST

To Wisdom

Sometimes what is foolish for the head may be wise for the heart.

WILLIAM BENNETT, EDUCATOR

A fool gives full vent to his anger, but a wise man keeps himself under control.

THE HOLY BIBLE: PROVERBS 29:11

Seeing much, suffering much, and studying much are the three pillars of learning.

BENJAMIN DISRAELI, STATESMAN

A wise man changes his mind, a fool never will.

SPANISH PROVERB

Life is a festival only to the wise.

RALPH WALDO EMERSON, ESSAYIST

The highest wisdom: Freedom and life are earned by those who conquer them each day anew.

JOHANN VON GOETHE, PHILOSOPHER

THE EVENT

THE DATE

THE TOAST

BEVERAGE USED

To Work

All of us want work that provides us the opportunity to grow. Growth in the business world should be financial, psychic, and personal. When we are committed to our work we will do it well. And when we do our work well, our families, friends, and fellow workers pay attention. As Studs Terkel wrote, “Work should help you in your search for immortality — to be remembered.”

To Work

"Now" is the operative word. You don't need endless time and perfect conditions. Do it now. Do it today.

BARBARA SHER, AUTHOR, LECTURER

It is not because things are difficult that we do not dare; it is because we do not dare that they are difficult.

SENECA, RHETORICIAN

Take a chance! All life is a chance. The man who goes the farthest is generally the one who is willing to do and darc. Thc "sure thing" boat never gets far from shore.

DALE CARNEGIE, AUTHOR, SPEAKER

The mark of a good action is that it appears inevitable in retrospect.

ROBERT LOUIS STEVENSON, AUTHOR

In order that people may be happy in their work, these three things are needed: They must be fit for it. They must not do too much of it. And they must have a sense of success in it.

JOHN RUSKIN, SOCIAL THEORIST

To Work

No-risk management run both no-win and no-fun businesses.

AL NEUHARTH, PUBLISHER

At any given moment, man must decide, for better or for worse, what will be the monument of his existence.

VIKTOR FRANKL, PSYCHIATRIST

I do not know anyone who has got to the top without hard work. That is the recipe. It will not always get you to the top, but should get you pretty near.

MARGARET THATCHER, STATESWOMAN

It's no good running a pig farm for 30 years while saying, "Really, I want to be a ballet dancer." By that time, pigs will be your style.

QUENTIN CRISP, WRITER

All work is empty save where there is love. And when you work with love you bind yourself to yourself, and to one another, and to God.

KAHLIL GIBRAN, POET, PHILOSOPHER

About the Author

Steve Deyo is a speaker, writer, and consultant who specializes in ideas and principles that apply equally to leading a company, an organization, or your personal life. For over 24 years he has been selling products and services both nationally and internationally. He created, published, and sold, "La Vista de Mexico," a newsletter on travel to Mexico. His work has appeared in the New York Times, USA Today, Travel Holiday, National Geographic Traveler, as well as business publications. He is a graduate of Miami University, a member of Toastmasters International, the Colorado Independent Publishers Association, and the American Wine Society. He believes that life is a great adventure that must be celebrated. There can be no more elegant way to celebrate your adventure than through an eloquent and enthusiastic toast.

Services Offered

Steve Deyo is a frequent speaker at national conventions and conferences where he conducts seminars on the Art of Toasting. He is available to teach this stylish art to your group, organization, or business. In addition, he writes custom toasts for any milestone event. For further information on Steve's lectures, seminars, and custom toasts, please contact:

Aventura Communications
617 Golden Eagle Circle
Golden, Colorado 80401
Tel: 303-271-1401
Fax: 303-278-1699
E-Mail: pepperdeyo@juno.com

www.theartofthetoast.com

Bibliography

Fox, Sue, Etiquette For Dummies, New York, NY, IDG Books Worldwide, 1999.

Post, Amanda, Emily Post's Etiquette, New York, NY., Harper Collins, 1997.

Conover, Jennifer Rahel, Toasts For Every Occasion, New York, NY, New American Liberty, 2001.

Dickson, Paul , Complete Book of the Best Toasts, New York, NY, Dell Publishing, 1982

Gresham, Perry E., Toasts: Plain, Spicy, and Wry, Anna Publishing Inc. Ocoee, Florida 32761, 1985

Vocatutus atque non vocatus, Deus aderit

(INVOKED OR NOT INVOKED, GOD IS PRESENT)